BENEATH
MY BODY ARMOR

BENEATH MY BODY ARMOR

POEMS BY

DAVID GLOVER

gatekeeper press™
Tampa, Florida

Beneath My Body Armor

Published by Gatekeeper Press
7853 Gunn Hwy., Suite 209
Tampa, FL 33626
www.GatekeeperPress.com

The cover design is by Shawn Carney. The editorial work for this book is entirely the product of the author. Gatekeeper Press did not participate in and is not responsible for any aspect of this element.

ISBN (paperback): 9781662921834

Author's Note

I must confess...I never intended to share these poems
with anyone else. I wrote this book because I wanted
to memorialize these moments and memories–in order
to get closer to my grief–in order to get closer to my
mother. I wanted to share with *her* my inner life during
childhood and young adulthood–that twenty year
period of her absence.

Early on in my adolescence I *knew*, no matter how
much I prayed for my mom to come home, that she
was gone and there would be no turning back. No
matter how, when, or *if* she returned. I had to let the
dream go. I had to do something drastic to save myself
from the pain–something that no one else could. I had
to kill whatever thoughtful conjuring of a mother I
ever believed I *should've* had. And so I did.

This death was swift, like turning off a light inside
myself. Later, I began to believe it was necessary
for survival, but this was false and simply my body's
response to housing immeasurable grief. The death of
that imaginary woman–*the mother I never had*–created
in me an imaginary life that is impossibly reaching,
yearning, to make room in my life and in my body for
the mother I do have. This book is an arm of that reach,
an elegy; a poem or song of mourning.

And like a restless thing in need of letting go, or a burden
in need of laying down, I know true rest can only be
found in forgiveness. And so my hope is that–although
this book was written solely for my mother–you may
also find yourself within these pages. And when you do,
may you find friends, family–perhaps your own memories
too–and maybe, just maybe, some forgiveness.

Contents

"...I forgive you. I forgive you. I forgive you."
from "Phase One"
Dilruba Ahmed

"Death and life are in the power of the tongue: and they that
love it shall eat the fruit thereof."
Proverbs 18:21

for my mother

Beneath My b o d y Armor

I. Unscathed

unscathed

Where-in / this / body

    Is / there / a / bo(d)y /un/bro/ken,

de-void/ of / armor?

II. Translations

Kindred eyes voice claims
Opening worlds of secrets
Only families keep

kind-ling

I know
What it is

To hold a dream
like a candle,

> for the dream,
> *like a flame*

To burn.   *I know*

What it *is*
To burn.

To watch   your *tongue*
    ablaze,   dissolve your life
              (*a breath*)

With nothing
           but
               your words

honesty

To tell the truth
Is also
To tell yourself
I love you

After the Fall

Explain the child
To the apple:
thin skinned, arborose, bulk of flesh
Hollow chord Seedling

Stem of nothing, attached
—to air, hungry
for Separation

From dust.

And those furtive hands
Always Reaching,
Occupational hazard.

Limbs in limbo
Body baby jello
And eyes—

Two certain
Lighthouses,
Scanning the rotund
Horizon—

Gaping mouth
Forbidden teeth
A simple galaxy
Of screams
Scratching
The vibrational language
Between looks

And the landing

Still in question
After the fall

Am I safe?

Are we safe?

And The apple

Hanging In there

No longer guarded, fingerling
greedily pried by
gravity's sacred promise

unable to ask the questions

Lynn

grandma's hands are bridges
large meals to traverse a meaty history
built and burned
like those ground beef burgers
sculpted between red sand palms,
cupped, like the whole world's in your hands
softening and thawing out
overtime

a smorgasbord of mouse droppings
ambience your cupboards
and the seasonal cup
I was looking for
to fill
With ice cream

Your wrists
doorknobs
Protruding into those 50+ years of marriage
Like secret rooms

My mother
Your only child
Enters,

Must have been
A trap,
door somehow

looking
older than you

lacuna

      Touch

of skin

                           and

            kin

and sin

               —an empty

unlike another's (void)

        —what is,

                the
              ultimate

intimate

On life terms

Sometimes,

When I regret it...

I don't stay long

Enough—to feel it,

Blister

Or if I do,

I do not suffocate long

Enough—to catch

A break

History : History

Or History

Repeats itself

My father exclaims

My father's father's words

"This is gonna hurt me more than it's gonna hurt you"

—if I am going to be a statistic

O how I want to be in that Number

17

of men who—when seeing the devil,

call on the name of Jesus

and not

their *mother*

Family

Generations of women
With histories heavier than time
Music in their limbs
Mourning in their sons
Laughing with words and crying with sighs

Do you know how we got here?
Do you know the reach of your grandmother's
footprints?

My mother's humor is swollen in my father's hands
A thousand sad songs laid
Open to the air
With our prayers

Dear heavenly father,

Brick by brick

We are rebuilt.

Inheritance

I know words may do little to salve

The trunk of heartache

But perhaps

The roots

Can use some

Affirmation

—

Stories of you have been the stones

A rogue memory's bedrock

The dirt and water mossed footage

Your actions, motion pictured

A dandelion sprouts out of the dug

Primal veiny misuse of rotten roots

Cleft at their bark

Unsheltered arterial children

Womb—Home—Mother—Earth

Parasympathetic nervousness

Ravishing salvations laughter

Time and again

Pulling me back

Extremities furled
Yarn locked baby
Umbilical necklaced
Don't Push!
Or PUSH

Whatever the commandment

No matter,
You saved my life
that day

You rest within my facets
double helix—eyes, nose, gap toothed smile
Dad's pictured too—in great relief,
the presentment of two souls
swaddled one
like some double dutch stitching
Dad says you met at a bar
I still have yet to memorize your number

I rest my eyes on a photograph of you
Ocular assurance that my inheritance
Is different than my siblings'

And why is the image "spitting?"

Is it sick?

Has it run out?

Will it leave me?

classy colorful boxer punchin'

for grandpop

Take these hands,

        morphed phalanges

stout with pulp and meat,

        blood and bone

cornmeal nail beds,

        wrinkled knuckles

puffed and bruised with,

        earthly conversation

thick hammers,

        when curled to bow in

promise to your palm.

Take these hands,

to gulp a beer,

to cook fried chicken,

to teach me how

to tie a tie

Those deadly weapons

Stiff with rigor mortis' grip,

clutching your swollen
twins

that old pair of boxing gloves,

coiled,

reddish brown,

weathered organ, singing

24

And that famous left hook,

                              with your knock-out
              laughter

Left right in the coffin there,

                    with you,

the coffin keeper's bell's rung

I remember the photograph

of my brother: Jonathan

preemie

floating in your palm

And oh, your hands,

able to hold;

a wife,

the life

you never had,

the daughter you did,

the six grandchildren,

the six great grandchildren

and counting

Translations

Hold

As long as you can

While he asks your mom questions

About her condition

her,

Swaddled in that aria

Of blankets and sheets, like a tongue

$\qquad\qquad$ *In that vacuous hospital bed*

That seemed in one gulp to swallow her,

—but couldn't, in fact entirely stomach it—

and choked on cooked spinach,

and those feet sunk somewhere beneath,

as if three stories below

$\qquad\qquad$ *in the earth*

$\qquad\qquad\qquad$ *in the grave*

tethered to the white oak in the courtyard

27

between hospital ward and bodega.

these two decades attest

the really good job she's done

of un-making beds—her children, in them,

the roots

head shrouded

     as in the habit of a nun

          Or the attire

               of a ghost.

As *she* shares with *You,*
Gregory, Jonathan and James
The parameters of her condition
The particulars
Particularly alarming

Mom begins,
          (*The interlocutor's mandate,*
          the purgatory patron's post,
          Schizophrenia's intermediate medium)

to verbalize another's response from within

                                          her body
                                          her body
                              (part) of my body

and I remember hearing *that* word
schizophrenia

When I was little
And the movies depicting
crazy people in mental hospitals
screaming at their nothing partners
holding chats
and ceremonies
for those without bodies

And I remember my body
In that moment
Beside my brothers
Side by side by side by side
Four leaf clover

As the robed physician,
a wizard,

Spells out the nature
Of her condition
With words I've only heard from foreign tongues

And I want to know that language
        I want to know my mom

29

                              I want to press rewind and remember
              how
we got here

And then I remember
Gregory's phone call two days prior
How I missed the initial call—his first attempt,
unsuccessful
because it was before 8am
And I was in college—

The peculiarly familiar exhaustion in his voice
That only comes from bearing unfortunate news
The respiratory alarm in my inhale exhale
from hearing about her *attempt*
fortunately, unsuccessful

my train ride to Broad and Olney
him picking me up
driving to his house
where she'd been staying to recover in sobriety for the
first time in decades

the heat of yesterday trapped in the stairwell to her
room
which used to be Kayla's

and the egg-white door that Greg flung open to reveal
a modest room

a dresser

some medications atop

beer cans—in brown bags—in black bags

coins and papers everywhere

                        the small window facing the
            backyard

the twin mattress with a white cliff hanger bed sheet

                holding on for dear life

                and me *(holding on for dear life)*

the big black trash bags on the floor

                like bulging heads of lettuce

stuffed in myriad ways with mom's clothes

                for every season

and in this season

                the litany of cigarette butts
                sprinkled throughout the room

like bird feed

                and the closet stuffed shut

31

and the butter knife

which had been used to make

her wrists and ankles   bracelets

to paint

the room

red

and so

we wrapped the semi-caramelized mattress,

   that sopping, pungent bar of soap,

in the limp arms of emptied severed heads of lettuce

we carried that RED planet
down
the stairs,

   pallbearers
   in orbit
   to the outside

and all the while

in that vacuous room

oldest and youngest brother,

rapt in fraternal silence

celestial

bodies

drifting

holding-on-to-each-other

gemini & cancer

as we clutched rags of shirt

knelt before God

took bleach to floor

and
attempted

to clear our maternal bloodline

III. Between Us

risk

Will you
Still *Surrender*
In the light?
-
{Your tongue danced this *question* on my inner thigh,
-
My *eyes* retort–
A tantric *silence*
-
You trace a *continent* onto my *spine*
Electric fingernails and *all*

I welcome the *tsunami* rushing there

-
South *cartographer*}

Amor

There is
No answer
That clots
The blood
To a pleading
Heart
Than to moor
The unmoored

Island

we sit on island
with water drenched
tear filled eyes
we be the sun by ourselves
you be the moon by myself

tapered land and crisscrossed lines
fight tidal waves
while stars dance on your bosom
wrinkles ripple these waters
we be the sun by ourselves
you be the moon by myself

we sit on island

and clouds like jungle gyms
play xylophones on your neck

and the wind whispers wildly

we be the sun by ourselves
you be the moon by myself

and we our island

Swingers

We'd be swinging here if forgetfulness hadn't lost our
love
And god hadn't forgotten our feet never touch the
ground

We'd be shifting back and forth
Traveling through time and running our minds amok

You would be grey
And I would fall
On your back
Like snow
And the leaves would wither once
And the wind
Blow

And the ground would crunch
And we would hold on to the swings

And they would know nothing
Of chains
And chimes
And the calmness that winter brings

universe

I saw you naked
Hair curled
Tighter than our fingers
Whirlwind bedsheets
Cringing
Knees captivated
Water between our webs

We catapulted
Red leather skin and burgundy eyes
Penetrating

Past the rainbow
Past the future
Past the galaxy
Past the freedom
Past the fortune
Past the rearview
Past the universe

This good

I whispered your name
into the universe

and it showered me
with answers

of how your laughter
and the blossoms
are one

and how the stars come out each night
to look for you

and when you finally appear
there is wholeness
and the healing begins

and you're warmer now
than I remember

and my memory won't always be this good
this good
this goodness
that you bring

I know the earth admires you
I know the earth admires you
I know the earth admires you

T.W.Y.H.M.

to hold you,
is to cradle
a peace of mind
your hands
a soft reminder of your strength
stable and secure
your beauty
a shadow of your heart's dwelling place
Your heart
a full moon
Your eyes
a window to the home that you are
reflecting
a home within
A resting place
a place of life
your voice
the mark of safety and intention
Your will
to choose me
I call you
and the tide pulls me closer
to your midnight
howl
outshining lunar songs
the way you hold me
as if
you have
within yourself
the blueprint

Colina

I wouldn't call myself a morning person
But I do believe we're breakfast folk

We always suffer warmth for the sake of it
Hot cakes and eggs, scrambled,
sub the meat for avocado

you are
and you are *home*;
colina

Worry

I wanted
To digest you
And place the portions
Of your gut I could not stomach
On the palace floor

I thought
If worry crept too deep
I would muster the courage
To feed it
You

When goodbye is goodbye
2013

I've been drawing circles lately
ominous things
deep around the edges
concave
introverted
and insular
circles
deep blue-black blotches that represent us
right now
but these blackened eyes have been clawing at
the idea of forgiving you
you
who mix-match
crisscross
back stabbed me

betrayal knows nothing of crucifixion
I stand here
the equivalent of
a bastard child
strung accordion style
across
a cross
wrists bleeding venom
blue black blood
tears shedding their poison
Pierced side and all
you weren't finding new love
you were mis-taken
You were driving the nails deeper

it smells like the sound of bricks breaking
it looks like the sound of raindrops
it feels like the sound of earth's quake
and taste like jumbled words

it sounds like I love you
it sounded like I love you
I love you
I don't know if I love you
I am less than,
whole
I am left with holes
Holier than thou

a breaking fleeting voice in the wind
and somehow now
I'm speaking louder than you

I've been trying to recover
You've been trying to redeem yourself

Thou preparest a table before me
In the presence of my enemies

but it's hard to forgive
when you've seen the culprit caught
and 65 will remain etched into my mind forever

for the number of times you emptied his Cup
for the number of times you refilled it
for the number of times you added distance between
us
for the number of times it runneth over
for the number of years my blood will run black not
blue

for the number of circles I've drawn
For the number of inkblots in my mind

If you ask me what the image is
Surely,
a conglomeration of fury rage and disbelief
shall follow me all the days of my life

it looked like adventure
running from home to him

it looked like death and its blackness walking beside
me

it looked like me caught
tug of war style between an ocean

It felt like a bat to glass bones
like heat to eye sockets
like a knife to my throat—choked

I have the holes in my hands to prove it
the holes in my feet to prove it

the cage for a heart hung out to dry in the sun
It's been wrung

leaking blue-black blotches
no penmanship can answer
puddles of confusion and questions

I couldn't find anything grand enough to describe how
much I loved you
so I said

I love you
like circle

when goodbye is goodbye
the sun will turn black
and the clouds will drape themselves
in an indigo sackcloth
and there will be no more loops
to noose me into believing
in love

Botfly

The wind whips screams through the cracks
in your window sill
As I scroll through Instagram
Screen too close to my eyes
While I search for parts of you to rescue
From your past
        And envy takes hold too
        As I witness the lasting joys that
        Traveled with you

Upon waking
You greeted me with a kiss
           And said I love you
then left
And I love you

And somehow wrote inside myself
A memoir of how unlovable I am
And I love you

And I contemplated suicide today
And I love you

Attempting to clean your room,
The parts of it I've frequently encountered
wishing a blessing
on your house

a blessing on
even the nieces and nephews with names so similar I
don't remember

you are good
with names

and the wind seems to be calling
your name
in the room
while I'm here
conjuring you

though every shared memory
has replaced me

shhh
it seems to say

shhh
as if to calm me into deep sleep
or self-worth

shhh
and I can decipher your desires

shhhhhh
semi-nestled and growing
like a botfly in the skin

and again

shhh

but this time
the pitch is higher
and it holds for a time
long enough to suffer a goodbye

and then
goodbye

unlock

Searching with my tongue
.

.

for, you're secret:
.

.

the locksmith,
.

.

Unwinding
.

.

your knot
.

.

The same
.

.

as me

Friend

And she blushed a world into existence

Her mere existence unfurled a whisper

      The leaves whispered

And a panoply of stars wished she caressed them

As if she alone could bless them-their bleeding hearts

      And she alone took twilight with her

With her they were remembered

Re-membered birds in the welter of royal winds

      And they bore wings of wisdom

And wisdom ushered them shelter

And they bore silent silken dreams

      Tethered tightly, watered sweetly, by
Egyptian streams

Like Egyptian queens they gathered

Watchful eyes and hearts were wasted

      While she noosed a smile

I heard the sun drip blood

I felt the moon move love

        I saw the sky across a rain cloud blow
rainbows and lightning glow

Thunder, comets, comics

And a sunshine moonshine show

        Mimicking panic

While wild animals ask wildflower fanatics if,

She was here

        And here she was

A Storm from nowhere
Everywhere she went she left

        An understanding of rebirth

Necessity made it so

My madness never knows

        When she's coming back again

I hope she's coming back again

She came in a dream of earth and wind

        Set a fire beneath my skin

And breathed me new life again

A friend

A friend

A friend

Derision

Forever will be your melody
I've contemplated your derision
For, how long will time be, remains the question
Still, remains the question

We were both borrowers
with a fist full of love and the tension within our
fingers to hold it
for how long remains the question

Maybe it ends
somewhere beneath the metaphors
or right before it reaches the heart
maybe it terminates—dies
or turns to Ashes

maybe it doesn't
maybe it doesn't

perhaps we can learn to dissolve fury and fate
or Bury it in some weakness we forgot we had

is it possible to unlove?

forever will be your anthem
for how long we were both borrowers
with a fistful of heart
and not enough tension
To hold it

Worn

Tell me a joke,
Like you used to
Cradle my laughter in yours
like water in your hand

Tell me,
I'm not forgotten
Hug me
like you used to
Like you're used to me
Lifting you up
Gasping for comfort
And air

Body sprawled like
Lovers floating
flower petals
A wishful hope of romance
And a future

Kiss the ego from my forehead
And wash me
Clean
Like you used to
Like you're used too

Tell me I'm not a memory
And if I am…

Re-member me
The way we were.
And how we never cried together

Remember all my parts
The hairlessness
The moles
The wide hips
The nose
The contacts
The wet
And the bruises

Tell me,
Have we made it this *far*
as *friends?*
did we un-earn
the lovers within?
did we uncoil that part of the covers?
are we cold?

my feet are

calloused
tired
worn

tell me
are you?

Are you worn?

Are we worn-out?
Of love? Or time?

Tell me you're sure
Tell me your shore

And I'll meet you
by the water

Hugging you
Seeing if it lands

dangerous game

it wasn't dangerous when our footsteps were etched in
these sidewalks

like most of us
love is in the foreground

it wasn't dangerous when our laughter was heard
echoing like angelic symphonies

like most of us
we didn't care who was watching

it wasn't dangerous when we stole for the sake of lust

like most of us
we were selfish
we weren't dangerous
of sacrifice or of honor

it wasn't dangerous to become defeated lovers
to become monuments
to be Frost

we were not dangerous.

we were, like most of them

read when listening to Yefikir Engurguro

for jasmine

Between us

between us
the two of us
twill and wool
one
by one
beside another
heart and heat
and blood
and breath
softening
like eggs
or ease
our
easiness

each
enter
inter-webbed
interweave
interwoven
intertwined
laced
interlaced
knotted
tangled
tied
trussed
pair
peers

appearing
a poem
a partnership
a second
a space
double
a balance
a bridge
embraced
embroidered
entangled
equal
equivalent
linked
coiled
corded
courted
couplet
counterpart
companion
company
compadre
leaves
floating
falling
tethered
to the ground
to the grasp
clinging
binding
both-halves
whole
whole worlds
wound
holding

whole worlds
whole wounds
whole wonders
holding
holding
we
us
team
matched
mates
yoked
you
and i
you and i
you and i
you and i
You
and I
You And I
dyad
duo
dos
two
of us
one
by
one
beside
another
holding

tight
tight

IV. This Dark Sculpture

there will be no pictures of pigs shooting down
brothers on the instant replay
there will be no pictures of pigs shooting down
brothers on the instant replay
there will be no pictures of pigs shooting down
brothers on the instant replay
there will be no pictures of pigs shooting down
brothers on the instant replay
there will be no pictures of pigs shooting down
brothers on the instant replay
there will be no pictures of pigs shooting down
brothers on the instant replay
there will be no pictures of pigs shooting down
brothers on the instant replay
there will be no pictures of pigs shooting down
brothers on the instant replay
there will be no pictures of pigs shooting down
brothers on the instant replay
there will be no pictures of pigs shooting down
brothers on the instant replay
there will be no pictures of pigs shooting down
brothers on the instant replay
there will be no pictures of pigs shooting down
brothers on the instant replay
there will be no pictures of pigs shooting down
brothers on the instant replay
there will be no pictures of pigs shooting down
brothers on the instant replay
there will be no pictures of pigs shooting down
brothers on the instant replay
there will be no pictures of pigs shooting down
brothers on the instant replay
there will be no pictures of pigs shooting down
brothers on the instant replay
-Gil Scott-Heron

VII

What's it gonna be?
One more Black boy shot, for what
Smelling the flowers?

IX

Abracadabra
I'm the cadaver screaming
All black lives matter

For the signs

I see the signs of the judgement coming lord
I see the signs of the judgement coming
I see the signs of the judgement coming lord
Hallelu Hallelu Hallelujah

Black moon hangs on the backdrop of black stars in
the night
and we call it darkness
Or rather,
Black man hangs from the bent branch of choke cherry
trees in the night
and we called it righteousness
But for the signs that read white only
And for the symbols that prove The black man's
journey,

> The black woman's
> journey,

> The black queer
> journey,

> The black trans
> journey,

Tiresome, weary, heavy laden,
There is no rock that will cry out for us
No Hebrew that can save us from the times
For the signs

I see the signs of the judgement coming lord
I see the signs of the judgement coming
I see the signs of the judgement coming lord
Hallelu Hallelu Hallelujah

The animals know when trouble is imminent
When danger is coming
The crawling things hide
And even the birds disappear
So why couldn't anyone notice when there were no
nests in the trees just black birds flying

I see the signs of the judgement coming lord
I see the signs of the judgement coming
I see the signs of the judgement coming lord
Hallelu Hallelu Hallelujah

They'd hang enough of us
The leaves on trees would turn to vines
And the branches would bend like limbs
And the screams would sound from a distance like
stifled cries
And they'd call them weeping willows

But for those still traveling
In an effort to escape
Burnt hands and feet
Broad shoulders
That extra bone that makes us faster
Jutting jaws
Thicker thighs
Bigger lips
deeper eyes
And blackness

They remain
Deeeeeeeeeeeeeep
White water washed
Wading
Waiting

Waist deep
Wasting away watching
White man
When we were
Wild men once
They took them
Thorn and throne throttled
Thrashing tumultuously
Thundering
Torched
Tombs ransacked
Drumbeat
Ran.
Run.
Beat.
ba ba ba
ba ba ba
ba ba ba
ba ba ba
BOON!

Running
Drenched
Doomed
Drained
Some died
Dried
It rained
Dancing
Destroyed
Desire
Distant bodies on fire
Disfigured
Frenzied feet patter

Fast Fast Fast
Fast Fast Fast
Fast Fast Fast
Fast Fast Fast
Faster

Following falsehoods
Frozen
Histories forgotten
Harmful
Heinous
Hardship
Slaveship
Hiccups
Heat bumps
And headstrong
Chased
Chastised
Crushed
Crash
Crisis
Cremate sons
Crim*son*
Cracked
Ceasing
Seasick
Semen stained
SOLD!
At auction
Silent screaming

Some prophets
Profit
Profess
yet seldom practice
however,

mix–match
tears
tears
tar
feathers
and
a nigga
and you've got yourself a big bird
a black bird
a black dove
swinging
hanging
dying
for the signs

Untitled

DIE

I am

                              Not
                         ready
                              To
                         die

                              I
                              Am
                              Not
                              Ready
                              To
                              Die

I

AM

NOT

READY

TO DIE

Iamnotreadytodieiamnotreadytodieiamnotreadytodie
Iamnotreadytodieiamnotreadytodieiamnotreadytodie
Iamnotreadytodieiamnotreadytodieiamnotreadytodie

I

                              AM

NOT

              READY

                                        TO
I

                        AM

NOT

              READY

                                        TO

76

In the Summer of 2016
upon waking from a nightmare
I grabbed my pencil and wrote
these words

Sweet nothings

I pursed my lips to kiss the barrel yesternight
I pulled the trigger
chewed the bullets
became the nigger of the night
and my mind took flight
and I took a fifth of Jack Daniels down 6 flights
then crash landed on a beach with three wild geese
and this duck duck goose chase got me feeling like,
meek
Mill cheap thrills
And she cockpit her head back
then downed angst and anxiety pills
I was type anxious when I tried to cop a feel
like David Copperfield
you couldn't see my hands
don't tell a soul
but the cops could tell I sold
and it's a sellout album
I'll bloom I'm sure
like the children of the night
that sprout from concrete jungles
encased in red rum brick houses
that have gargoyle leaped from the ledge
and Section 8 themselves to Infinity
Infinity : Infinity's beyond me
but I've been there before
besides beside me she lay light like lilies

lavishly laced lucidly liquored in a gown of fine wine
and wisdom
I pondered all the questions I'd never ask her, like
why come I can't take the Nigga out of my skin?
And when I'm gonna be free?
and why come we ain't free?
she
traced a cratered moonstone on my heart center
took me through time like magic school buses do
and whispered
sweet nothings to me
sweet
nothing's to me
and nothing's to me like I and die
are one in the same
I sank deeper into myself
like turtles in an expanding Galaxy with dwarfism
issues and Benjamin Button disease
I pondered jazz and contemplated Kendrick
I tried to Limn my thoughts
but my mouth wouldn't start
Stop
Telegraph to forgotten niggas,
Stop.
I surmised I hadn't been woke
Stop.
and a nigga remains a nigga sarcophagus wrapped if
he isn't awakened
stop.
If he hasn't Jordan leaped to reach Nirvana
Stop,
or nothingness
nothing less than nothingness will do
so, I packed my scarlet letter shirt
and went searching for answers like Winnie the Pooh

and found you
honey
you seemed otherworldly to me
and my earthling mind can only half orbit around
your monumental fingers
your caress was something between
the psychedelics of Grachan Monchur III's trumbonal
wind wizardry
and strange fruit
I've spent Holidays with you
and every day was a holy day with you
you'd teach me things like rhythm
and the Blues
we had syncopated heartbeats that would Richter scale
into oblivion
We had kisses that lasted like wind chime solos
like 3.14159265357589323 and on
We had romance like Roman candles popcorning in
the night
and I wonder
Is there a ribbon in the sky for our love?
OR
Is it cornbread
butter slick
smooth whipped screamed
I can't believe it's not?
I can't believe it's not?
I can't believe it's not.
CLICK
and the weasel goes POP
mind blown
Exposed
neck hairs rose
the remnants of an artist's soul
half shown

Scattered
like we breadin' chicken
But man cannot live by bread alone
now
free to roam
I went searching for you
in another home

Inside

this grief
like my blood
runs through me
and I weep
all of the time
inside

X

Were all my wishes in vain
Were all my musings for naught
Did we dry up the rain
When the battle was fought

Can you hear them calling
Are those whispers of the dead
Or lucid bodies falling
From the bullets they were fed

Make the ground swell bleed
Take the roots from the soil
Hear the fell trees breathe
And the corpses extol
From the soul

We were here
We were here

We were here

XI

And where is all my joy?

Stowed away
Or stolen?

In some steel wool
Young bull
Hoodie
Or a safe?

A keepsake of safety
Never
Keeping safe

And though I breathe
When even on misty days I can still see
Through the trees

Taking in the
forest,
foliage,
the leaves

Thinking black jewels can be won

I wonder
how many rounds per son
Does it take
To take a
Black boy
Black girl
Black or brown person

Brownies

And these the blessed children

Do roam the streets of Jordan
Do climb the walls of *Jericho*
Do walk towards *heaven's* gates
Babbling for connection

They speak a thousand thoughtful *tongues*
Wear weary clothing where there were none worn

These the blessed children
Do drive in droves to the *divine*

And somehow,
come up short

Only to find
Their souls
Drenched in time

And ain't God real?
And ain't these God's blessed children?
And don't they
got a say
in the matter?

Closer

You came into the world,
Fists tight,
Each finger
Kneeling,
Trying to get back to
The bone.

I entered
Palms toward heaven
An offering
Aching open
Like a wound

And then
I remember
How *black* absorbs the sun
And *white*
Pushing back
Reflects it

IV

And BOOM from the womb
Joyful black baby is born
Does it have a—SHOT!

V

White Mass Murderers
Are always being treated
Better than my kin

I want to die of natural causes

I want to die of natural causes

But

"natural"
causes
white
folk
to

do
some
crazy
shit

some
crazy
shit

some
crazy
shit

some
crazy
shit

some
crazy
shit

warped

Caged at four corners

Black skin. Black men. Alien.

There's no camouflage

VIII

Men, always looking,
always looking for something,
something they can break.

R.F.

-after Robert Fuller

I chew the glass
and swallow tongue
the blood congeals
with cheek and gum
I throat the words
and all is numb
I pray to God
thy Kingdom come

the world is rot
with whited spot
and blackest death
that won't be stopped

and blackest death
that won't be stopped
that won't be stopped
that won't be stopped

roadkill
-after Michael Brown and David McAtee and others

To *carry* something
Like *water*, in a bucket
Or a pot
Or even a spoon
Can be a *difficult* task
Depending on the *quantity* of water
And the *capacity* of the object *bearing* it

And *yet*
The body bears *water*— *Yes,*
This body too—
Something like 62%
Of its *composition*

But,
dehydration is the loss of water from something
and to *drown*, is to die through *submersion* and
inhalation of water

And *also*
The body's *ability* to bear *water*
Is not *equivalent* to
The body's *ability* to bear *bullets*

And Is not the body a *planet?* Orbiting other *celestial
bodies*, testing its gravitational pull.
The earth, something like 71% *water.*

Is not the body a *building?*
A house; or home?
To *carry something.*

To *carry* something—*sizzling*
Like a *dehydrated* body,
or a *meal*—Microwaved *too* long?

And that body-*there*. Too. That home, *flooded*
with bullets. And the *sound.* That sound that makes
things thump and fall.
—*snap, crackle, pop*—

kettle corn body

Abandoned. Dried up
Still heating the *road/kill* with nothing
but another gravitational force upon it

When we meet the air

What is the skin
But a vintage badge
clothed in flesh and bone
a story cloaked in thread
generation after generation
What do we ask of our bodies?
when we meet the air?
does it recoil?
like the chamber?
does it barrel down on us?
S
H
O
T
shot
dead
shot dead
shot by dad and son
Shot *from* life
shot from *life*
to death
shot to *death*

Before breakfast
August 23, 2020

Bless your beautiful hide; Or, The last poem I shall ever write about the death of someone that looks like me, due to police brutality
-after Jacob Blake and Emmitt Till

I do not watch the news anymore
Instead I grandfather clock the views of the poor
write incantations through meditation & revolutions
for the Moors
Furthermore,
I implode and implore more empathy-morality-for
impure peeps
who sight see police brutality without question in the
streets
these streets whose hearts are set on the American
dream: immortality
I, one mortal man, as you sight me, recite poetry
as so to tally more totally, the totality of my mortality
I write poems at vigils and eulogies
with no apologies
Saw wavelengths of the almighty
Kungfu fighting the adversary
Principalities above the firmament
This is for all the humans
All new masculine and feminine energies are
welcoming
Oh Yes, I've been grandfathered in
but
The news

Yes, The news is never good
The news is never gospel, so to speak
I'm slow to speak
When the blues repass my being asking me to
Witness-sing
their funerals

I'm always like "don't nobody bring me no bad
news"
And the news is always bad
The news is never new
The news is old
The news cycle
Follows the same life cycle
Of a young black kid killed
Trying to learn how to ride a bicycle
That's one chance today
Or two cycles
with three strikes against you
For every wheel cycling
That's 3 squared now
before riding
So now were fore-running
Usain bolt or grease lightning
recycling
Nine lives all cats lives matter
Abracadabra I'm the cadaver screaming all black lives
matter
10 degrees of separation from the bullets splatter
6 feet under for social distance
7 shots out back for Mr.Blake,
8 thru him like a ribeye steak and black eyed peas on
the dinner plate
and yet he still alive

it's a miracle
but he can't ride a tricyle

Tri*cycle*
Hand cuffs
And feet locked then
Try shackles
Try escaping the grip of a white knight
Death Factor-y

The news is after me
The news is *after me*
Like menus
Hello, welcome to America, may I take your life?
In a patrol car following me
In a park following me
In the night following me
In my sleep following me
In my dreams following me
Happy Holloween
Hollow tip ready to hollow my body
Before breakfast
Let us pray
Hallowed be thy name
Before hello
Before my hide is blessed with the kiss of death
And why is it a kiss?
And why I gotta hide?
Kiss of death
Perhaps they know I pursed my lips to kiss the barrel
yesternight
Perhaps they're far right
Perhaps the barrel is a mouth
The tongue a knife
the bullets spoken word

And what they gotta say?
The bullets say...
The bullets say...
they know that breath is the entrance to the soul
And blood is the goal-d standard
And yes they're waiting for the hiss of the body
de-flating your soul's answer
a battle to clean the heart and soul of America
but The souls of black folk
Run black like black soap
To wash the black soles of black folk
From running this fuckin race

And I'm tired.

Perhaps it's in the water, or underground
Perhaps it's in the power of vibrational sound
perhaps they know of being violated
assaulted, degraded, accosted or the *price* of
assimilation

this land is your land this land is my land
and the tunes wound through gun sounds wound
and the wounds are never one
and the battle is never won
—too many
one is too many and a thousand is never enough
hello?
how many bodies to fill your quota?
Wrong number!
Enough
Hello?
When are words enough
Enough is enough when it's word for word

But when the reverb disturbs your listening perhaps
she's only heard
On the undercurrent

My ancestors heard her through ticks in the clock
Perhaps you've heard of her
Tick tock tick tock tick tock tick tock
Hip Hop
Time is running out

my eyes have seen the glory of the coming of the lord
dressed in *blue,*
white hoods hunt hooded blacks *read:* hoodlums
from the hood
but you were there first under hoods
hiding
your fear of being seen riding head to toe in all your
whiteness
the birth of a nation
write this
on my hide as you skin me
blesss your beautiful hide
wherever you may be
we ain't met yet but I'm a willing to bet you're the gal
for me

and though drums are hollow
Their guns too are hollow

They'll try to drumbeat me to the grave

And everything else
Follows:

Black folk like boneless shadows

Swallowing the marrow
Yesterday Today and tomorrow
Targets narrow to the point that arrows
So the writing begins from the harrow
And do your torture
Or do you torch her?
Or him?
Or do you remove the drum skin
stickin' to my guns
From the drumstick
Grip your guns quick
And unload a clip
Into a youngin
White Folks grab your collard greens and
watermelons
Black your faces in celebration
No black out spaces on your phones or televisions
The revolution will not be televised
Will not be televised
Will not be televised
Wll not be televised
The revolution will *be live*
Believe
I live the recurring revelation of a lie
All men are created equally a lie
But some shall thrive
and others be swung from a bootstraps noose in the
sky
dripping blue black blood that'll blot out our eyes
that we may see things clearly, nearly
and Dearly

Dearly beloved, we have gathered here today

To get through this thing called life
Electric word life it means forever and that's a mighty
long time
But I'm here to tell you

It ain't no mystery I'm missing
Tallahatchie River deep
Cotton gin
Bedridden
Nooses be my boost over the fence
Coil me colored
Old language
Black
I have yet to learn to float by my free will
Screaming FREE WILL
AND EVERYONE ELSE
Now we ain't got no voices left
We standing in the streets cus they ain't got no breath
Screaming I can't (breathe)
It cost too much

For my wedding
Me and bullet gettin' marred-married
Mary Magdelene type bedding
Be my whistling witness sista
I'd look a sponge like me if I be missin'
Listen
Connor, bull—
Let's bullets dance the bachata with many black souls
1950's type music
I wouldn't be caught dead
Wearin' that dress

Wherein that they dress me like a martyr
Hoodied

I knew one Martin,
Trayvon
Wherein they killed
Murdered like martyr
Trayford Pellerin
Killed. King. Killed
Medgar. Martin. Malcolm

bbbddddddddddrrr
A New Year has be gun
Jan. you airy as fuck
Chk.chk.
Close enough to be my birthday
Cheese
They killed me and asked me to smile
They shot me and told me to die
They drowned me and bade me to fly
They shot me

Face looks like a net
I mean Emmett
Face looks like a microscopic view of a fly's eyes
Till
Face textured like a sponge
Holy beaded brow
Holy ffff
(inhale)
I can see the sun through him

Let your light so shine before men that they may see
you're

Black

Wipe that look off your face

Nervous?
You sweatin' bullets

The bullets say
You was malleable
The bullets say
You was easy to work with

The bullets say
Bless your beautiful hide
Wherever you may be we ain't met yet but I'm a
willing to bet
We
Will

Sometimes,

rage surfaces

without warning

when I am out

in the world

The mark of end times

I am the harbinger of our Armageddon
Striking revolution with every echo of our footsteps
Pulsating Through breakbeat boom boxes
permeating through oxygen
Our Genesis begins here
raptured in the cortex of my frontal and temporal
lobes
my vision is slightly off kilter
because I've spent too much time with Helen Keller
tracing the words in your palm that are to me
like dancing constellations
my limp, is synonymous with the gait of an amnesiac
cripple
torn between the presence of his legs
and their inevitable immobility
my speech is like the stuttering stammering lunatic
society's cast away
because his only proclamation is apocalyptic in nature
make way
make way
for surely the end is near
for surely you remember
Balthazar's banquet
the writing on the wall
the seventy sevens cycling 666 times
way up in the middle of the air
the mark of the beast
the mark of end times
the mark of blood moons
the Lake of fire
144 thousand
the exodus
Leviticus

numbers
Deuteronomy
Joshua
judges
Ruth
first and second Samuel
1st and 2nd Kings
first and second chronicles
Ezra
Nehemiah
Esther
Job
psalms proverbs Ecclesiastes
Song of Solomon Isaiah Jeremiah lamentations Ezekiel
Daniel
Hosea
Joel
Amos
Obadiah
Jonah Micah Nahum Habakkuk
Zephaniah
Haggai
Zechariah, Malachi and for the millions more who will
neglect his claim
make way
make way
for surely the end is near
they'll say, *he sounds like the man on the corner*
you know, old man wilson
caught in the mix match dimension between yesterday
and forever
but every day is a nightmare for him
purple and red are synonymous
blood boiling open wound futures
he is a lurker

he sees everything
because his four by four eye vision yields him 6 trillion
eyelids
enough so, so that his pupils are the stars
every time he blinks it thunders
boom: flashbacks to times past when we were past our
limits
boom: mentally fixating on the structure of your frame
boom: your framework is screwed, too much has
passed through your system
and now your bench broken back must carry this
message to your friends
he bears the hands of a Carpenter
the wit of a comic
the sense of a soothsayer
the timing of the tooth fairy
and yet *he* is personified by *I*
so *I am* the only witness to this misfortune
and I am *that* I am
trail mixing beats with the thump of hypnotic music
breadcrumbs of his ecstasy

With the forethoughts of reason rhythm rhapsodic
righteousness
his only message—*my* only message, is that of
repentance
make way
make way
for surely the end is near

this dark sculpture
-after George Floyd

As with
the pewter air cascading about the body cavern

As with
the mucus blood lengthening porous veins-tumult

As with
the mettle fascia upholding briny sinew downward

As with
bones

As with
music and measure

As with
graves and the deep-deep

As with
chimes and falling trees gregarious

As with
striking avalanches of anemia

As with
the rolling hills and rotundas tunnel out on dope

As with
the metamorphosis of cellular life
and the decadent decay of mortals

As with mortality

As with conundrum
and cicadas

As with rhyme
and rhombuses

As with the trap house
—the trap and the red lined house

As with reconstruction,

As with destruction
and dessert

As with tumor
and time

As with the north star
and the spangled banner coming with

As with culture
and espresso shots-*fired*

As with cheese

As with gluttony and mutation

As with maturation

As with the bullet
and the bullet holder

head,

       neck,

gut,

       wound;

the trick that got the bullet caught

—cramped ruthlessly betwixt the eye

and the bridge of the nose.

As with toy soldiers felled to this conundrum, as well.

As with gun in mouth

As with hope

As with holding breath

As with hoping for death

As with death notes

As without life

As with death sentences

As with ellipsis

As with…

As with…

As with the puncture of a dart through epidermis

As with blood drawn

As with weapons too

As with the sonic nature of fright afoot

As with your life running amok

As with mockery

As with morose and mores

As with no more

As with intentional institutional malintent

As with,
the maraca clatter of sprayed *death sentences*

falling clad and softly, on the ground—providing
balance to the body felled a foot away—filling

The pewter sky with red reflection,

for good measure

a few more bullets added to this dark sculpture

whose blood wanders aimlessly
seeking a north star

The body hissing its final circadian rhythm
metamorphosed into
a second

life
hugging the earth

clinging

for the hope of death—sooner
than time

As with all things dying
expressing that sacred want

—to live

V. Beneath My body Armor

the wound

                              tend
                           to the
                           wound,
                         not seen
                            with
            corporeal   eyes the wound
               that   does   not
            smell   as putrid   on

    the   out   side

                         the wound
                      that hasn't felt
               noticeably   picked at
                  but   all the while
               in broad   day l i g h t
               reaches   i t s
               h a n d
               beneath
               t h e   d i n n e r
               t a b l e
               a n d s   l   o   w l y
               v a n q u
                   i s

                                      h   e   s

    y   o   u

116

A Photograph of Myself

See the Boy
In darkness
The indigo of his jumpsuit
Sharing the soft green halo
Reflected by nearby footlights

Behind the eyes
Pupils thick and dilated
A single tear
Leading a hajj
Rivers down the right side of his cheek,
The smallest waterfall.

His face
Stone like
In its rigidity
Brown
Jaw tight
mouth shut
shrouded in
a spectacle of hair
standing at its ends
like torch bearers, mountainous.

Beyond the boy
In the background
A strip of luminous neon light
Borders the thin embankment
Of a box he stands within

An apparatus hovers hazily
In the distance

Behind the left shoulder,
of the boy,
nearly imperceptible,
besides a few shiny red and white lights
in the blur and
yet somehow connected too
to the boy, who
stands so close to the edge of the image,
running, from what
(the foreground hugging him)
It's as if,
You can almost hear him
Cry

Brotherly love

there were a thousand of them
kids screaming
in the schoolyard parents too

red brick face house
dad said he called the cops on the drug dealers
long block
the same block
the same block
10 years ago
and probably
the same family 10 years before
black
Bard
school on the corner
mostly white teachers
gone at three o'clock sharp
red
orange
fire hydrant
water
clears the air of dumbos

listening for cops
and he be selling on the corner
sitting stooped looking stupid on the corner
and young boy shot on the corner
walking home from school
far removed
from my neighborhood

black boy
in a sea of gremlins
bold enough
with a violin strapped to his back

Cold stone

Kaleidoscope optics
Peek-a-boo

Body bubble wrapped
6 yr. old burrito

Internal organs mix vegetabled

Pot-hole eyes

We hit a pothole!

Swerve left

We've stopped now

He unraveled my ragdoll body

Took a two by four to the scalp
   Unfamiliar combing

I don't remember my conscience
I don't remember being a part of the group

Or the taste of blood

Salt, iron, iodine, gasoline skewers and the block party scene

I just remember,
The *knock-knock*, who's there?
Of a familial face
The relative feeling of forced hands
On private parts

The pulp of my teeth in a burgundy black mouth—after
eating the curb

The chicken bone pop of my elbows

The crack of my wrists being tied

> *I'm double jointed now*
> *I'm broken black*
> *I'm cold stone*
> *I'm ruined*
> *I'm beneath death*
> *I'm almost gone*

We're on the highway now
My brain's in a blender
We've stopped now
On the off road of a back road

I hear the metallic click of the trunk,

> *Or my bones,*

> *Or a gun*
> *My blood's wrung*
> *I can see the sun*
> *I can see his eyes*

He looks familiar
He looks like me a little,
Relatively sick and a bit young

The drapes close

The blinds shut and blind

> *I know*
> *I know*
> *I know him*

alike

House with thickest smoke
Seized in the rime of earth
From birth
These crazy tombstones

. . . .

I've never seen a blade of grass as dull
But I've seen you
Lynched there
With your head slumped
Wilted son-flower

. . . .

You weren't a man long enough
To know the difference
Between the barrel
And your head
The round and the shotgun sound

. . . .

—alike

. . . .

The blackness and the grey yard
Or the graveyard
Or jumpsuits—or oranges,
Or orange jumpsuits

. . . .

You weren't a man long enough, to know you were
ripe, fruit cake
Or that birthdays come with age
In fact,
Around this time last year
You were hanging around here
Slumped
Next to your friends with three strikes against you

Keep me by the sun

The flower grows and is plucked,
Like black pepper from my teeth. I remind myself
their journey is different than mine.

The stemmed orphan—cut at its ankles,
finding a way—to listen—without roots
To the water beneath.

Closer now
To drink
And easier—*to drown*
But that won't happen

Because someone will choose me
They'll pick me up
And take me home
I will be the cause
Of their joy
Not a thing
to pry between teeth

I'll be centered
In some room
Near a window—for all the Birds
to wonder how
I levitate.

—About my wounds;
They were given to me,
And I carry them
—In my spine
At the edge of my being

I've seen a few magicians
salvage my brothers and sisters
            —a way to live—post
rot,

                dry as roots
                Or bones

            I am assured
There is a second kind of life
When wetness has left our lips
And relief tastes like silence
and we begin to shed more easily

                Even so,

        Keep me by the sun

Secret

they don't know it yet
my eyes aren't black they're blue
my lashes are longer than usual
but my contacts aren't see-through
but I am

I am
I am rainbow
I am yellow
I am gal
I am beguiled
But there are no smiles inside

He makes me
Warmer than she did
He makes me
Grunt
He makes me
Feel pretty
But they don't know it yet

My shoulders are much more slender now
My frame is much more weak

And I can't seem to count
How many guys this week

My back arches deeper now
My hips are much more wide

But I still got that thing dangling between my legs

My knuckles don't bruise
With blush or a crush
But they don't know it yet

My nails are red
My lips are red
But I'm comfortable in the closet

Tick Tock
2012

Tick tock
Tick tock
Tick tock
Tick tock

Hip hop is
A ticking time bomb
But she's currently only heard
On the undercurrent
That's the radio station that exploits her
Tick tock
I mean, plays her
Tick tock
But who's to say she's been up long enough to know
the difference

Or,
Perhaps she hasn't been up
Or perhaps she's been back down
Or bent down
Or back down on her knees again
Tick tock
She makes a mighty noise the way she blows that
trumpet
T   i   c   k   t   o   c   k

And she's really been blessed with the lungs of angels
Heaven sent
Even though she
Hasn't sent me new music
Hasn't sent me new tunes
Tick tock

Hips lock
Tick tock
Hips rock
Tick tock
Pop lock
The heavy scent of her womb

Tick tock
Tick tock
Tick tock
Tick tock

Hip hop is a ride-or-die bitch
And I know she's gonna die
I'm just trynna hit
I hope she wears that sundress again
Still got that ass
Them wide eyes
And that soft skin
I hope she wears it often
And since we're headed to my place
I hope she takes it off then
I hope she's not a nuisance
Wanna talk about memories
And being a kid and shit

I'm just trynna hit and dip
And get this bitch to suck my dick
And go so far until we quit
And go so far until we quit

Hope that she's
Down for whatever
And not worryin' what her mother thinks
I hope that cannabis is her friend

131

And that she loves to drink
I hope that she can dance like a ballerina
And don't care that it's a full moon
Or that it's more than just me in this room
Or that it's more than just me in this room
I hope she has enough room in her womb for all the
wannabes
I hope that this is what she wants to be

Tick tock
Tick tock
Tick tock
Tick tock

Hip hop is a monster
With legs spread like horizons
But her eyes aren't as noble as suns
Or daughters
But she has arrived
She has arisen
She has arisen
She has a reason
to be the spirit wrencher that she is
I bet that she has kids
With some illegitimate man with the hands of a
woman
Kin
He prolly be her mannequin
They kids prolly be retarded and started pre-k three
times and kindergartagain
They prolly wearin' cardigans
They prolly spit when they speak every now and then
they pants prolly sag when they walk
And they got a limp

They prolly soaked in confidence
And violence

And sirens
And Tupac
And Biggie
And new balances
An imbalance in these kids
And you'll see them standing like flamingos or
Ostriches playing hopscotch
In concrete landfills
In the same places that birthed these kids
Tick Tock

But she's currently only heard
On the undercurrent
That's the radio station that exploits her
Tick tock
I mean, plays her
Tick tock
But who's to say she's been up long enough to know
the difference

Hip hop reminds me
when the clock strikes three
to behave nicely
cus this world dislikes me
and poetry is not free

it's ugly
disfigured
betrayed
horrific
obnoxious
unconscious
hypnotic
prolific
I get it, I'm wit' it

Tick tock
Tick tock
Tick tock
Tick tock

Hip hop is a ticking time bomb

Tick tock

But she's my time piece

Tick tock

My dime-piece

Tick tock

And I be watchin' her

In the garden

Begonias
Lilies
Roses
Daffodils
Weeds
Crickets and things
Soft feet
Stomping on worms
The dog got loose again

Attack the lilies
Attack the roses
Keep the weeds

I imagine
When I was a child
I could ride atop that furry beast of a dog
And conquer
Explore
And sometimes destroy

Grandma's garden

A-way

Where are you going?

                     Somewhere far

Tell me?

                     I love you

Tell me something?

                     I love you

Tell me something Real?

                     something real?

…

I love you

                     Tell me something

I love you

                     Tell me

I love you

Rejoicing

there is a place
between the gospel
and the hymn

a place of testimony
            testament

In the church
The black church
Before the singing has begun
The musician will play
the sounds will rumble and swell

and in this space

of preparation and possibility
The saints will summon God

So by the time you open your mouth—

        You in the choir,
        You in the pew

—The space is filled

And in this place
where blessings flow
where feet can stomp
where hands can dance
and bodies witness

Here,

I reside

A witness
on the edge
Feet dangling from the verge of a pew
Unable to meet the floor with,
this grounded understanding

of how the song is sung
    how it is belched like fire from the belly
    how it is raptured in the air
    how it is felt in the bones
    before it touches the ears

And my soul tries to cry Hallelujah

But I am shy
and young.

Though,
there is a fire shut up in my bones
I do not want
to embarrass myself

this,

is a political act
a kind of resistance, to make
distinctions
between
My soul's rejoicing
and my body's comportment

this,

is the first sin
   the first neglect
of self

In this way
I begin the lifelong process
Of swallowing
Of { }allowing
Myself to look outward-in
And say "what will they…"

So,
I learned to shrink
To fold myself
In half, in half, in half
In half, In half, in half,
In half, and have
Little for myself,

Yet,
Within that tight and darkened space
Where blessings are sung
In silence,
I worshipped
And when asked by Deacon Alexander
    "what song you got on your heart today,
brother?"

I deflect,
    "you know I got a song on my heart, but what
song you got on yours?"

Sure enough
He'd answer,

And I would leave him empty
though he would leave me filled

And he never sang all that well,
But he knew how to rejoice

    he knew his testimony

    he'd often shout hallelujah

                              I never let out one
                    hallelujah

And now,

Because of this,

when I worship
It is mostly in silence.

when I suffer
It is mostly in silence.

Yet,
in this silence
I can hear the chorus of hallelujahs

                              I am *unfolding*

in this *narrow* silence
There is still a song

Yes Lord,
There is still a rejoicing

good mourning

In the *mourning*

Where secrets sleep sound

The alarm

Wakes me

And all my worry freezes taut

Untaught how to wonder full

Of grief and longing

The boy beneath my body armor

before he opened the door
I knew
it was over
that all my wonderings
had been washed away
like some forgiveness
I heard his clipped footsteps
ringing like hallelujahs in the hallway

the gap between the floor and the base of the door
spit the faintest of light into my room
I swallowed my breath
closed my eyes
bit my lip
searching for the answered
prayer

his footsteps sang louder
as my heart repeats the same knock
on the door as he
knock knock
knock knock
his knuckles against the wooden door
a stark friction

The kind that is required
when conjuring fire

he knocked again
But still,

my body couldn't answer
the call

and in this stillness
between barrier and him

the boy
Beneath my body armor

silently
hushes my fear

to freedom
oh, the man I will become
the
one I must
become

A past-present,

to soothe the child from

What makes a healthy relationship?
What do we need?
What's important to us?

What do we want it to be?
Where do we want it to go?

Write it down.

one

Ancient bodies of water
calling out
are you there?
bodies of woe?

bodies of woe
bodies of travelers
have you sacrificed?
have you surrendered?

I ask, what have *I* to do with the saving
of bodies
of water
bodies a blood?

bodies wholly holy
whole enough to see through
bodies hollow barren
War torn
And white
with fear
are you ghosts?
is the haunting done?
has the hunting begun?

Bodies wailing
petroleum sheen reflecting
bodies of promise

I promise

loud bodies
braggadocious bodies

branded bodies
bodies built on
Broken plans
Braved, brined and beaten Bodies

Behold
breathtaking bodies of water
all about us
flowing
from one body
to the next
spilling open
Omens into itself
crashing
ceaselessly
again
and again

One body
swoosh

one body
swoosh

one body

There must have been joy

I don't know the end of this story
But during the night
I often try to end it
This is not,
A good thing
That every day is different
And I am different
Everyday
Though I seek the same dependable guarantee aloneness
perpetuates

In the beginning
There must have been joy partnered with the weeping

How else could we have still survived

VI. On the Rise

On the Rise

I stand at the precipice of some great great moment
in history and I'm looking out over all the people and
they're far away from me but there's an element in the
air that seems to pull them closer though I can't see
their faces and they look like dots or…ants but the
distance doesn't seem like a gulf between us more like
a river and I'm at the top of this…this mountain-like
thing and I can see I can see all the things the birds
the trees the oceans the fish the buildings the roads
the people all of it and I feel this warmth this…intense
warmth like the tops of your feet stepping into a hot
bath and this feeling encompasses my whole body
bathing me in this glow and it is bright it's really
really bright so bright I feel like smiling even though
I'm dreaming I feel like I can see the face of God and
I close my eyes so I'm not blinded but it don't make
no difference when I do that 'cause it's still the same
just as bright as before—if not brighter and it's about
this time I start getting a little scared 'cause I figure I
can't escape this light and I definitely don't wanna go
blind no thank you I'll take hearing loss 'cause even
a deaf man don't want to go blind so I go to open my
eyes but…but all of a sudden it's changed… it's all
gone…just like that…darkness—complete and utter
darkness—darkness so dark you can't even see those
fuzzy white dots in your mind—darkness so dark
it's called pitch and I can hear something some*one*
breathing this heavy heavy breathing and I hear the
sound all around me now like a siren and I hear people
around me breathing heavy too and they're moving
towards me—encroaching—so I start kicking to
catch ground so I can run, 'cause I've been floating
this whole time, but I'm not moving really or if I am

152

I can't see where I'm going and I start screaming I
start screaming but it keeps coming out like a whisper
and I'm really frightened and scared 'cause the
breathing is getting louder and louder and closer and
closer and I'm frozen and in that moment like a man
possessed I start praying I mean praaaaayyyyiiiiing
hard and asking God for forgiveness for *everything*;
for the things I did when I was a kid till now, the
things I knew of, the things I didn't know I did, the
things I thought— 'cause I be thinking some crazy
stuff sometimes, stuff only God and I know—and I'm
crying, then I realize that the breathing is *me* that I
can like...hear *myself* breathing and the tears are still
coming but, I'm alright, I'm not scared anymore and I
focus real hard on my breathing and it starts slowing
and all of a sudden It's quiet—pitch quiet—just like
this...and then it's bright again and I'm not afraid
anymore and I can see everything...I'm not alone in
the dark...it's bright...and I know you're there

Acknowledgements

Abounding thanks to Dilruba Ahmed for permission to use a quote from your book of poetry, *Bring Now The Angels* in the beginning pages of this book.

No book exists without the cosmic and practical investment of brilliant humans working together. Although I could not possibly name all the people who had a hand in the making of this book I will name a few whom this venture would have in many ways been impossible without. Thank you to the New York Foundation of the Arts for granting me a City Artist Corps grant which provided funding for the publishing of this book. Thank you to all those at Gatekeeper Press who had hands and eyes on this book throughout its development, especially Jennifer Clark. Thank you Shawn Carney for saying yes to this project so early and designing the amazing covers. Immeasurable gratitude to Mrs. Warner, Dr. Kimmika Williams Witherspoon, Jennifer Kramny, my late mentor; Lee Kenneth Richardson, Ms. Collier, Elsa Johnson Bass, Marlene Goebig, Dennis Weiner, Valerie VanPham and the countless teachers, staff and students in the Philadelphia Public School system who ushered me into a greater love of language and self expression.

Special thanks to; BABEL Poetry Collective, Temple University Poetry as Performance and Poetic Ethnography Classes of 2012 & 2014, CAPA HS Class of 2011, Culture Lab LIC, and my entire church family at Faith Fellowship Baptist Church (I love and miss you).

A heartfelt thank you to the angelic human and shining light that is Nasimiyu Murumba, who introduced me to the community that was The McCarren Gathering from 2020-2021. Abounding thanks to Keepsake House, thank you for welcoming me, sharing your artist friends and resources and fully supporting me. Deepest vulnerable thanks to Alex Wong and Sarah Kang, you already know.

An avalanche of thanks to my poetic peers, loves, comrades and artistic collaborators from the earliest days till now; Anwar Johnson, Cambriae Winifred Lee, Leilani Myers Doyle, Mitchell Edwards, Angel Clardy, Natyna Beans, Joshua Wilder, Jana Henry, Carvens Lissaint, Beau Thom, Rand Faris, James Whitfield, Nisha Venkat, Keishel Williams, Shawn Carney, Ebony Kennedy, Miranda Cohn, Trevor Bayack, Sophie Blue, Mel Chante, Kerri Blu and the many others who I am endlessly grateful for who've shared their passion, art, and fearlessness in vulnerable spaces with me. An ocean of gratitude and thanks to Jasmine Pierik who shared many poems with me and encouraged me to write this book and for whom several of these poems were written.

Thank you to all my poetic inspirations, peers, elders and ancestors whose works inspired many of these poems; Saul Williams, Maya Angelou, Lucille Clifton, Aja Monet, bell hooks, Toni Morrison, Jericho Brown, Angeline Cazeau, James Baldwin, Yrsa Daley Ward, Dick Gregory, Richard Wright, W.S. Merwin, Forrest Gander, Gerald Barrax, Ocean Vuong, Dilruba Ahmed, Rupi Kaur, Louise Glück, Reginald Dwayne Betts, Layli Long Soldier, Morgan Parker, Claudia Rankine to name a few.

156

A lifetime of thanks to my best friends and chosen family; Dana Hawkins and Brandon Ballard, Grace Pauley, Polina Ionina, Weronika Wozniak, Tana Sirois, Ilker Oztop, Steven Lamont, Monica Koh, Ji Hae Byun, Bryanna McQueeney, Lauren Smith, Paul Styer, Georgia Miller, Elizabeth Chappel, Garrett Turner, Bonita Jackson Turner, Doron Mitchell, Kirin Tubo, Darliin Khahaifa, Keenan Tyler Oliphant, Jamar Brathwaite, Dhari Noel, Miranda Haymon, Michelle Williamson, Jarvis Green, Sandra Manzares, Ameerah Briggs, and Bibi Mama. Thank you for holding me, hearing me and rooting for me!

A deep thank you to all my friends, lovers of words, and masters of languages, who have shared with me your tunes, your music, your word songs.

Thank you God!

Unending gratitude to my family of origin; my first home, sanctuary, and audience. Especially my siblings; Gregory, Johnny, Kara, James and Nicole (& Tia and Nadirah) you are as much a part of this book as I am. Thank you for being my team!

Incalculable thanks to my Dad who taught me to mean what I say and say what I mean. You're the greatest man I know—your wisdom, integrity and love of God sustain me. Grandma Hopkins, there are no words that can encapsulate what you have given, what you have shared, what you have sacrificed. You taught me how to speak the words, the importance of memorizing and how to tell a story. I am forever indebted to you, our matriarch.

To my late Grandpa, James Harrison Hopkins, thank
you for singing loudly.

Grandma Taylor, thank you for powerful prayers and
for believing in me, I love you. For my Aunts, Uncles,
Cousins, Nieces and Nephews you are my everything.

And Mom, thank you for bringing me safely into this
world, for fighting for your life and coming home.
We're still here and I love you.

Notes

I   Unscathed

"unscathed": This poem disrupts haiku structure with
a syllabic structure 5-8-5. In order to correct this
poem the reader must remove a syllable from the
second line. Changing its meaning.

II   Translations

"Kind-ling": This poem is an admission and indictment
of what happens when speaking up and the profound
consequences in the loudness of silence.

"After the Fall": Taking the expression "the apple
doesn't fall too far from the tree," this poem draws
on the semblances of fruit/offspring and themes of
longing and connection.

"Lynn": My maternal grandmother's middle name is
Evelyn. My mother and my sister share the shortened
middle name Lynn. This poem examines the minute
changes that occur in the bloodline.

"Lacuna": The word lacuna means "an unfilled
space or interval, OR a missing portion in a book
or manuscript." Incest is defined as "human sexual
activity between family members."

"On life terms": This poem takes its name from a
phrase my father often says "life on life terms." This
poem reflects on lineage and the passing down of
abuse (beatings) which were often a way my father
chose to chastise my siblings and I. The quote *"this
is gonna hurt me more than it's gonna hurt you"* was not
only what my father would say to us before a beating,

but it is also what his father said to him as a child, before he was punished.

"Inheritance": This poem was inspired by my curiosities about genetics, lineage and Forrest Gander's poem "Son."

"Classy Colorful Boxer Punchin'": This poem takes its title from a story my late grandfather (James Harrison Hopkins) would tell. My grandfather was a boxer in his heyday and he would regale my siblings and I constantly with tales of this article written about him describing a fight he won with the title "Classy Colorful Boxer Punchin'".

"Translations": This poem is based on true events and was written in Fall 2020. I first shared this poem at a virtual poetry event, shortly after I received an avalanche of calls and emails from attendees which inspired me to share *Beneath My Body Armor* with the public. I shared this poem in collaboration with musician Alex Wong in 2021 at Keepsake House's *From Story to Song*. Now this poem co-exists with a companion song entitled *"Second Generation"* which appears on Alex Wong's latest Album.

III Between Us

"Colina": This poem takes its name from a restaurant in Crown Heights that my former partner and I frequented.

"When Goodbye is Goodbye": This poem was written in Dr. Kimmika Williams Witherspoon's Poetry As Performance Course at Temple University and was performed in 2014. This poem directly draws on my first romantic relationship and heartbreak.

"Friend": This stream of consciousness poem was written while listening to live Jazz at *Father Knows Best* in Brooklyn (2018).

"Derision": This poem was written while at Temple University in Dr. Kimmika Williams Witherspoon's Poetry As Performance Class and was performed in 2014. The Manuscript compiled at the end of class took its title from this poem.

"Worn": This poem was written in the Fall of 2019 after completion of my first polyamorous relationship.

"Between Us": This poem was written in 2019 for my partner at the time. It was written to be read aloud while listening to Yefikir Engurguro by Hailu Mergia. Excerpts of this poem have been in staged productions of *My Favorite Person,* in 2021 at Culture Lab NYC and at HEREArts in 2022 (with no music accompaniment).

IV This Dark Sculpture

The poetic influence for many of the performance poems in this section is Saul Williams. These poems have been performed at protests and poetry competitions in Philadelphia and New York.

"Quote": This quote is taken from the poem and song, *The Revolution Will Not be Televised,* by Gil Scott-Heron.

"VII": In May of 2021 officers arrested a 6-year old black boy who picked a tulip from a lawn at a public bus stop in North Carolina.

"For the Signs": The gospel refrain sung throughout this poem was the inspiration for this poem in addition to Billie Holiday's recording of "Strange Fruit."

"Sweet Nothings": This poem was written in the middle of the night shortly after the murder of Freddie Gray. It appears in my debut play *The Wanderer*, which premiered in NYC in May 2023 at The Chain Theater as part of the Short Play Festival: Time And Time Again.

"V": After being taken into custody for the murder of nine black people in a church in Charleston South Carolina, police officers bought Dylann Roof a meal from Burger King.

"R.F": "Black people don't hang themselves from trees, given our history, if we gonna kill ourselves it's gonna be quick!" Twitter user @taurusk_ posted on July 14, 2016. Robert Fuller, a 24 year old black man was found hanging from a tree in Palmdale, California on June 10, 2020.

"Roadkill": David McAtee was a beloved community member and the owner of YaYa's BBQ. He was shot and killed when police and the National Guard opened fire on a crowd that gathered in a parking lot. Louisville Police left the body of David McAtee on the street for 12 hours. This poem appears in my debut play *The Wanderer*, which premiered in NYC in May 2023 at The Chain Theater as part of the Short Play Festival: Time And Time Again.

"When we meet the air": In February 2020 Ahmaud Arbery, a 25 year old black man and former

162

highschool football standout was chased down
and murdered by Gregory McMichael and Travis
McMichael (Father and Son).

"Bless your beautiful hide: Or, The last poem I shall
ever write about the death of someone who looks like
me due to police brutality": After Jacob Blake and
Emmett Till. In its original form a portion of the last
two pages of this poem existed as a separate poem.
That portion was written in 2017 and was added to
the end of this larger poem, which was newly written
for performance at the McCarren Gathering Poetry
Night event "Black to the Future" in Summer 2020.
This is the longest poem I have ever written.

V   Beneath My body Armor:

"A Photograph of Myself": This poem is based on a photo
taken during the Off Broadway production of *In the Penal
Colony* at New York Theatre Workshop in July 2019.

"Brotherly love": In 4th and 5th grade I attended
McCall Elementary School in the central part of
Philadelphia. This poem is inspired by the years I
lived in North Philly at 1523 A. North Gratz St. when
I learned to play the violin and Trumpet.

"Cold stone": This poem was written for an
assignment in Dr. Kimmika Williams Witherspoon's
Poetic Ethnography class at Temple University and
was inspired by an article I read in 2014 about human
trafficking.

"Secret": This poem was written at Temple University
for an assignment in Dr. Kimmika Williams

163

Witherspoon's Poetry as Performance class. Inspired by the prompt "write about a secret."

"Rejoicing": I shared this poem in collaboration with musician Sarah Kang in January 2023 at Keepsake House's *From Story to Song*. The song entitled "*Little David*" was heard for the first time that evening.

"The boy beneath my body armor": This poem is based on a recurring dream I have.

VI On the Rise

"On the Rise": This long form stream of consciousness poem was written in 2018 as I reflected on a dream.

BLACK

I am black - the color of the street; the color
  of the panther that eats and eats.
I know that I'm not a slave because like
    Martin Luther King and Harriet Tubman,
    I know that I am brave.
I'm the color of the ink in a pen; the dye that
    makes ebony - the color of my skin.
Martin Luther King may be in his grave, but I
    know he wouldn't be a slave.
I know what Martin Luther King was trying to
    create.
I can relate.
Black is the color of the midnight sky; the
    color of your ashes when you die.
                David Glover
                copyright 2002

David Glover is a poet, playwright, actor, and director
from Philadelphia. Poetry is his first artistic love and
has been his most intimate artistic expression for over
twenty years. He is interested in stories that exemplify
the full complexity and measures of black life, love,
and liberation. His artistic body of work primarily
centers identity, history, and home. He holds a BA in
Theater from Temple University and has a passion
for horticulture and pottery. He resides in a lush plant
filled apartment in Brooklyn.

This is his debut book of poetry.
IG: @sirdavidlawrenceglover
acting: www.actordavidglover.com

Made in the USA
Coppell, TX
19 August 2023

20542198R00109